D1238232

AUTO TECHNICIAN

By Chris Jozefowicz

Content Adviser: Tony Molla, National Institute for Automotive Service Excellence

Gareth Stevens
Publishing

Please visit our web site at **www.garethstevens.com.**
For a free catalog describing Gareth Stevens Publishing's list of high-quality books, call 1-800-542-2595 (USA) or 1-800-387-3178 (Canada).
Gareth Stevens Publishing's fax: 1-877-542-2596

Library of Congress Cataloging-in-Publication Data
Jozefowicz, Chris.
    Auto technician / by Chris Jozefowicz.
        p. cm. — (Cool careers: cutting edge)
    Includes bibliographical references and index.
    ISBN-10: 1-4339-1955-9   ISBN-13: 978-1-4339-1955-8 (lib. bdg.)
    ISBN-10: 1-4339-2154-5   ISBN-13: 978-1-4339-2154-4 (soft cover)
    1. Automobiles—Maintenance and repair—Vocational guidance—Juvenile literature.
    I. Title.
    TL152.J72   2009
    629.28'7023—dc22   2009002343

This edition first published in 2010 by
Gareth Stevens Publishing
A Weekly Reader® Company
1 Reader's Digest Rd.
Pleasantville, NY 10570-7000 USA

Copyright © 2010 by Gareth Stevens, Inc.

Executive Managing Editor: Lisa M. Herrington
Senior Editor: Brian Fitzgerald
Senior Designer: Keith Plechaty
Produced by Editorial Directions, Inc.
Art Direction and Page Production: Paula Jo Smith Design

Picture credits: Cover, title page, Masterfile; p. 5 Harold Hinson Photography; p. 6 courtesy ASE; p. 7 age footstock/Dennis MacDonald/Art Life Images; p. 8 Hola Images/ Getty Images; p. 10 Art's Automotive Systems Manager Chris Strohm; p. 11 Associated Press; p. 12 Jupiter Images/Thinkstock/Alamy; p. 15 Justin Sullivan/Getty Images; p. 16 Mike Booth/ Alamy; p. 18 Schlegelmilch/Corbis; p. 19 Harold Hinson Photography; p. 21 Don Mason/Corbis; p. 22 Staff Sergeant Bill Lisbon/Department of Defense/ZUMA/ Corbis; p. 23 age footstock/John Burke/Art Life Images; p. 25 Everett Kennedy Brown/ epa/Corbis; p. 26 John Klein/Weekly Reader; p. 27 EVX Team; p. 28 culture-images GmbH/Alamy

Printed in the United States of America

1 2 3 4 5 6 7 8 9 14 13 12 11 10 09

CONTENTS

Words in the glossary appear in **bold** type the first time they are used in the text.

CHAPTER 1
ROAD READY

Most fans thought Clint Bowyer's race was over. The **NASCAR** driver got caught in a jam after 79 laps. His car hit a few other cars. The crash damaged his hood.

But Bowyer had mechanics in his **pit**. The mechanics fixed his hood and changed his tires. "The guys did a great job on the car," he said later. He fought back and finished in fourth place.

"To wreck and finish fourth," Bowyer said, "that's how championships are won." He was right. He won the championship for the NASCAR Nationwide Series of races for 2008.

Technicians at Work

Today, automobile mechanics are called **technicians**. They do much more than fix crumpled race cars. They fix the cars that people drive every day. They repair buses and trucks. They keep construction equipment and even military vehicles in working shape.

Technicians work wherever vehicles need care. There are more than 250 million motor vehicles in the United States. Keeping those cars, buses, and trucks running means a lot of work for technicians!

NASCAR driver Clint Bowyer (right) talks with his crew chief Dan Deeringhoff before a 2009 race. Find out more about Deeringhoff's job on page 19.

Technicians also help drivers bring some style to the road. If you've ever seen an off-road car race, you've seen what technicians can do. Cars with special tires, engines, and bodies all start in a technician's garage.

Cars Meet Computers

Today, all new cars come with some computers. The computers help control things such as the brakes and the engine. They check to make sure everything is working properly. They also control a **navigation system**, which gives directions to the driver.

These computers and electrical systems have turned mechanics into technicians. Technicians still tighten all the right parts and pound a bumper back into shape. Now they also use the latest in electronic testing equipment.

Is Automobile Technician the Job for You?

- Do you like to work with your hands?
- Are you good at taking things apart and putting them together again?

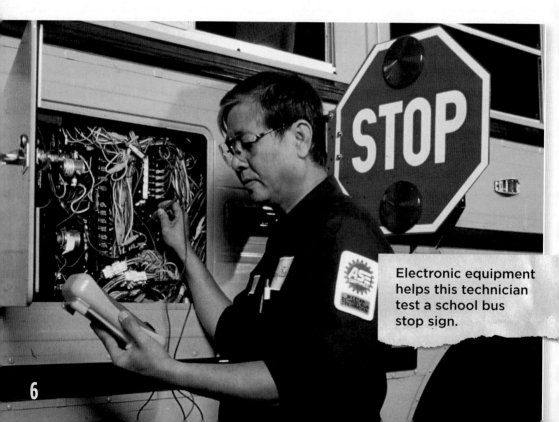

Electronic equipment helps this technician test a school bus stop sign.

- Are you interested in math, computers, and electronics?

- Do you like solving problems?

If you answered yes to these questions, this career might be for you.

Getting Trained

Many people start working in a repair shop after high school. They may have taken **vocational** classes such as auto shop in high school. Other people study at a technical college or trade school.

Many cars come with built-in navigation systems to help drivers get around.

Working on cars can be hard, tough work. Sometimes the hours are long. Technicians can start out making $15 to $20 per hour, however. With experience, they can double that amount. If they keep up with changing technology, they can count on finding new work, too. More and more vehicles drive America's roads every year.

CHAPTER 2

WHAT DO AUTO TECHNICIANS DO?

Can you picture an auto technician? Technicians on the job usually have dirty hands. That's because they use their hands to fix the cars. They take pieces apart and put them together again. But repairing and replacing broken or worn-out parts is only part of their job. Today's auto technicians do much more.

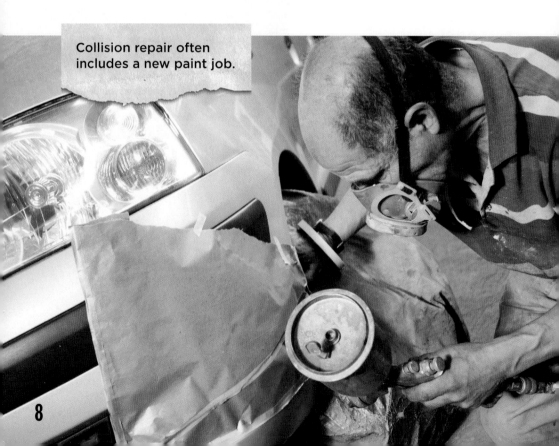

Collision repair often includes a new paint job.

Types of Work

What types of work do auto technicians do? There are a few main kinds of work.

Basic car repairs or normal maintenance is called **service work**. This work includes fixing an engine or brake system or changing the oil and filters. Collision repair and other **bodywork** involves mending a car's body. Technicians who do this work fix dents and replace broken bumpers after an accident. **Fabrication** is making special or new parts. Shops that specialize in race cars, construction equipment, or other off-road vehicles do this kind of auto work.

Some auto technicians do all kinds of auto work. But many technicians are **specialists**. They only work on certain parts of a car. Or they may only work on certain kinds of vehicles. "You have to specialize," advises auto shop owner Matt McCormick. "Find something you do better than anyone else and do it."

General Auto Technicians

General auto technicians work on all types of cars. They need to know how different car systems work. They must also know about many kinds of car models, as well as old cars and new cars.

General technicians do basic repairs and normal maintenance. They often work on the brakes and the engine. Many hold one or more **certifications** from the National Institute for Automotive Service Excellence (ASE).

Many general technicians have gotten their experience from working on the job. They may have graduated from a training program in high school or college. They know what parts and tools they need to fix the most common

On the Job: Hybrid Mechanic

Auto technicians are always learning the latest technologies. Art Ratner runs a repair business that specializes in cars powered by gasoline and electricity, or **hybrids**. Ratner says auto technicians have worked hard to keep up with new technology. "Cars used to be relatively straightforward," he says. "As they got more complicated, we had to get advanced training." He hires technicians who trained at a trade school and know computers. He also looks for experienced technicians willing to continue training.

These technical college students are training to work on a race car crew team.

problems. Very few technicians can fix everything. General technicians may direct drivers to specialists who can fix more difficult problems.

Special Attention

Specialists often work on a particular part of a car. They usually hold ASE certification or have factory training in a special kind of repair. Technicians must pass a test to get any ASE certification. Many very good mechanics do not have this certification, however.

Auto technicians specialize in many types of work. Here are a few of the common specialties.

- **Collision Repair:** Collision repair technicians work on the parts of a vehicle that might be damaged in an accident. These specialists repair car bodies, frames, and some mechanical and electrical systems.

- **Transmissions:** When technicians fix a **transmission**, they work on the part of the vehicle that sends power from the engine to the wheels. A car's major gears are in its transmission.

Some auto technicians specialize in car brakes.

- **Steering and Suspension Systems:** Other specialists fix the **steering and suspension systems**. Those are the springs and shock absorbers that connect the wheels to the car body. These are also the parts used to guide the vehicle. Steering and suspension systems help the car ride smoothly. They allow the driver to control the car safely.

- **Brakes:** Brake specialists fix worn or faulty brakes.

- **Engines:** Engine specialists repair the engine and its systems. The engine gives a car power and controls the air that comes out of the tailpipe.

- **Electrical Systems:** Electrical systems specialists do everything from wiring a car's lights to fixing the computer systems that control the engine.

Make and Model Specialist

Some specialists choose to work on certain kinds of cars. They may repair cars only from the United States or other countries. Or they might specialize in specific brands, such as Fords or Toyotas.

These specialists often offer excellent service. They have more knowledge and special tools or equipment for a particular kind of car. They know more details about how specific cars work. Some technicians also specialize to attract business and stand out from general mechanics.

CHAPTER 3

AN AUTO TECHNICIAN'S TOOLS

A car is not a simple machine. Open a hood and take a look at the engine. You'll see cables, belts, tubes, fans, and other equipment. Newer cars have one or more computers. These might be behind the dashboard, under the seats, or in the engine compartment.

To do their job, auto technicians must know a lot. They must know how cars work and how they break. They must also know what tools and parts they need to get a car driving again.

Street Smarts

One of a technician's most important tools is his or her brain. "Use your head and not your back to fix a car," technicians often say. They learn about cars in many different ways.

Some technicians get their training on the job. They never took a class about fixing cars. They started out

Have you ever wondered what makes a car engine run smoothly? That's the work of auto technicians.

working at a repair shop or garage. They swept the floor and took care of the parts and tools. These workers learned by helping more experienced technicians.

Other technicians took car repair classes in high school. They learned the basics there. Or they took classes at a community or technical college. Some of these schools offer two-year programs in auto technology. Students usually finish with an associate degree.

Some technicians started out studying auto repair in high school.

Educated students may be able to begin their careers at more advanced levels. Classes along the way always help technicians keep up-to-date with advances in the field.

The Toolbox

Auto technicians need good training. They also need a well-stocked toolbox. Auto technicians have four groups of tools to help them.

- **Mechanical Repair Tools:** All technicians have their own toolbox. It holds basic hand tools, such as hammers, pliers, and wrenches. It also might hold simple **diagnostic** equipment, such as pressure gauges, to help find out what a problem is.

    Technicians work with many powerful tools that belong to the shop where they work. Some tools use air pressure to power wrenches and saws. Shops also have special lifts to raise cars off the ground.

- **Body Repair Tools:** Technicians who work on the outside of a car have their own tools. They may use hammers to tap out dents. They use sanders to smooth rough metal. They also have special tools to apply paint. These technicians often operate special diagnostic tools. For example, frame repair equipment tells them if a car's body is bent.

- **Fabrication Tools:** Some technicians make their own parts with special tools. Fabrication technicians have equipment to join metal pieces to one another. They use power saws and drills to cut through tough materials.

- **Technical Equipment:** All technicians use simple test meters to measure a car's electrical systems. The meters measure electricity in wires and check if the car's **sensors** are performing properly. With the most advanced diagnostic equipment, a technician can check the communication between a sensor and a car's computers.

Many technicians use a laptop connected to a car. They might also use computerized test equipment that connects with a car's computer control systems. This computerized diagnostic equipment can help find problems. A technician can reprogram a computer-controlled system, like the one that controls a car's engine. This keeps the engine running properly and efficiently.

Many diagnostic tools use computers. These technicians use laptops to check the electronics on a race car.

On the Job: Crew Chief Dan Deeringhoff

Dan Deeringhoff is a NASCAR crew chief. He led Clint Bowyer and Richard Childress Racing to the 2008 NASCAR Nationwide Series championship.

Q: How did you get started working with cars?

Deeringhoff: I was always interested in motorcycles and cars as a little kid. Once I first started working on them, I was hooked.

Q: Do you need special training to become a NASCAR mechanic?

Deeringhoff: You definitely need it in our sport now. The cars are so technologically advanced that engineers have degrees. [They] have worked hard in school to be a NASCAR mechanic.

Q: What's the best part about working in the pit?

Deeringhoff: Winning.

Q: What's the worst part?

Deeringhoff: Losing!

Q: What helped you get to the level that you're at today?

Deeringhoff: Hard work and dedication to the goals I set. Also, the guys I have around me — the ones in the shop.

Q: Do you have any advice for young people who might want to become auto technicians?

Deeringhoff: Keep your head up and stay in school. When you're done with schoolwork, look for opportunities to start fixing your friend's bicycle. Eventually, find the opportunities to help out with working on cars.

CHAPTER 4

WHERE DO AUTO TECHNICIANS WORK?

Technicians work in different types of repair businesses. About 30 percent of technicians work in independent repair shops. About 30 percent work at **car dealerships**. The rest work in gas stations, city bus repair shops, and other places.

Car Dealerships

Technicians at car dealerships usually work on cars that are not very old. New cars come with a service **warranty**. Owners take their cars under warranty to the dealership to get them fixed for free.

Dealership technicians are very experienced at working on the types of cars their company sells. They work on the same kinds of cars all the time. They get technical service information from the companies that make the cars. Dealerships have many of the special tools and parts necessary to fix the kinds of cars they sell.

Many auto technicians work in service garages at car dealerships.

Independent Repair Shops

Some independent repair shops are part of big companies that have a chain of stores. Others are independently owned. Independent shops are often owned by technicians who have worked their way up. Successful independent repair shops offer high quality work and friendly service.

Independent repair shops often perform basic repairs and service work on cars. But independent shops are also where people go for **custom parts** and special work. Many repair shops now have the same tools and diagnostic test equipment that garages at big dealerships have.

Other Places to Work

Large companies often own many vehicles that require care. These companies hire technicians to repair their cars and trucks. Technicians also work for rental car or trucking companies.

Local and state governments also have a large number of vehicles. Technicians who work for the government repair police cars, fire engines, school buses, and snowplows.

Military Technicians

A mechanic in the U.S. Marines adds metal bars to a Humvee headed to Iraq.

Some technicians find training and work in the military. The U.S. military's Humvees, trucks, and tanks need lots of skilled technicians to keep them running.

Many technicians who serve the armed forces are members of the military. These technicians may work on a base in the United States. Others travel to war zones where the United States has troops and vehicles. When they finish their time in the military, their training helps them get a job in an auto repair shop.

Many Motors

Technicians use their skills to fix more than cars. Many auto technicians like working on bigger vehicles. They fix trucks and buses. These technicians know a lot about monster motors. Trucks and buses have special suspensions and transmissions. Their engines often run on diesel gas. Most cars run on gasoline.

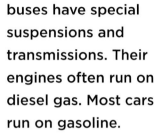

Technicians also apply their skills to planes, trains, and more. With training and classes, technicians can specialize in vehicles that range from motorcycles to motorboats. Even NASA (National Aeronautics and Space Administration) hires special technicians to work on their spacecraft.

CHAPTER 5

EXTREME TECHNICIANS

Technicians are creative. They have to be to solve problems and fix cars. But many technicians do more than fix cars.

These auto technicians are artists. Their art is a car or truck. They do special automotive work. They put custom parts in and on cars. Creative technicians change how a vehicle looks or performs. They often do this work as a hobby or as part of a general repair business.

Beautiful Bodies

Some drivers want a car that looks cool. Have you ever seen a car with shiny wheel rims or neon lights? Technicians have taken normal cars and changed their bodywork.

A lot of bodywork, like a colorful paint job, is just for show. Other bodywork changes how a car drives. For example, a shaped bumper can improve the way the air flows around a car. It makes the car move faster.

Technicians take their work seriously. This expert buffs a new paint job at an international competition for auto technicians.

Springy Suspension

A suspension system usually helps a car move smoothly over bumps in the road. But some drivers prefer unusual suspension. They want to change the way the car moves when it turns. Technicians can help drivers change their suspension. Some technicians even put in powered suspensions. These cars ride very low to the ground, ride on three wheels, or even bounce.

Motor Muscle

Technicians have solutions for drivers who have a need for speed. Technicians can change how the engine runs, to give it more power. When the engine produces more power, technicians must often change other parts in the car. They have to make the cars strong enough to handle the new engine.

Clean Machines

More and more technicians are helping make cars that are better for the environment. Drivers want cars that use less gas. They also want to power their cars with fuels that produce less pollution than gasoline.

This school bus uses waste vegetable oil for fuel.

Technicians of Tomorrow

Tomorrow's auto technicians are learning about technology's future today. High schoolers at the Academy for Automotive and Mechanical Engineering in West Philadelphia won their first "clean fuel" award in 2002. They won two more awards with a souped-up car that used clean fuel technology to go from 0 to 60 miles (0 to 97 kilometers) per hour in five seconds. "We want something that's cool and fast and still gets good gas mileage," said team adviser Simon Hauger.

In 2009, the students set their eyes on the Progressive Automotive X PRIZE. The prize goes to vehicles that travel 100 miles (161 km) on 1 gallon (3.8 liters) of fuel.

A technician can help turn a gas-burning car into one that burns natural gas or **biodiesel**. That's a fuel that comes from plant oil or animal fat. Some technicians have even turned diesel cars and trucks into vehicles that run on leftover cooking oil!

It's a lot of work to keep an old automobile on the road. This Alfa Romeo Giulietta Spider dates back to 1955!

Old Becomes New

Some technicians specialize in restoring cars. They use all the tricks and tools of service work, bodywork, and fabrication to keep old cars in driving shape. Most old cars are simpler than today's vehicles. But powerful new tools can help with old cars, too. Restoration technicians may need to make parts themselves because old parts are no longer manufactured.

Whether fixing classic cars or cutting-edge hybrids, technicians can look forward to a busy future. More and more vehicles will need skilled workers to fix them. Technicians who master the latest technology will keep their careers cruising down the road.

AUTO TECHNICIAN

OUTLOOK

- The U.S. government predicts that the number of automotive technician jobs will grow by 14 percent between 2006 and 2016. That's faster than average job growth.

- New cars have more electronic systems. Technicians with training in electronics and computers will have the best opportunities.

WHAT YOU'LL DO

- Automotive technicians repair cars, trucks, buses, and other vehicles.

- Technicians work with their heads and their hands. They must be able to discover what's wrong and then fix it.

- Most technicians work at an independent repair shop or a car dealership. Others work at government garages, gas stations, and car rental or trucking companies.

- Some technicians specialize in specific car systems or certain types of cars. Others make cars faster, stronger, or more environmentally friendly.

WHAT YOU'LL NEED

- Technicians can get on-the-job training. Many technicians study at high school automotive training programs or technical colleges. Most jobs in automotive repair do not require a college degree.

- Some states require a license to work as an auto technician. One way to qualify for that license is to earn ASE certification. Some states require a license to perform certain repairs.

- Repair work can be physically demanding. It may require long hours.

WHAT YOU'LL EARN

- Some jobs pay less than $10 an hour. But technicians usually earn between $15 and $20 an hour. Experienced technicians can earn more.

Source: U.S. Department of Labor, Bureau of Labor Statistics

GLOSSARY

biodiesel — a fuel that comes from plant oil or animal fat

bodywork — the act of making or repairing the outside of a car

car dealerships — businesses that sell new cars and service the same brand of cars

certifications — documents showing that the holder has met certain requirements

custom parts — parts that are made specially for a car repair

diagnostic — helping to find out what is causing a problem

fabrication — making new or special parts for a vehicle

hybrids — cars powered by gasoline and electricity

NASCAR — National Association for Stock Car Auto Racing; a stock car is shaped like a car found "in stock" at a car dealership

navigation system — a computer in cars that finds the car's location and plans a route using satellites

pit — an area on the side of a racetrack where technicians fix cars

sensors — instruments that can detect changes in an environment

service work — basic repairs or normal maintenance for a car

specialists — people with special skills

steering and suspension systems — the springs and shock absorbers that connect the wheels to the car body as well as the parts used to guide the vehicle

technicians — workers who use technology to repair vehicles and construction equipment

transmission — the part of a vehicle that sends power from the engine to the wheels

vocational — related to training for work in a trade

warranty — a written agreement to fix a product for a period of time after it is sold

TO FIND OUT MORE

Books

Banting, Erinn. *Inventing the Automobile.* New York: Crabtree
Publishing, 2006.

Gigliotti, Jim. *Fantastic Finishes* (World of NASCAR). Mankato,
MN: Child's World, 2009.

Sutton, Richard, and Elizabeth Baquedano. *Car.* New York:
DK Children, 2005.

Thompson, Lisa. *Pop the Hood: Have You Got What It Takes to Be
an Auto Technician?* Minneapolis: Compass Point Books, 2008.

Web Sites

Career Voyages: Student Information

www.careervoyages.gov/students-elementary.cfm#automotive
Watch videos about body repairers, auto technicians, and
motorcycle mechanics.

Collision Kids

www.collisionkids.org
Play games and learn about some cars at this site from
I-CAR Education Foundation.

National Automotive Technicians Education Foundation (NATEF)

www.natef.org
Find career information and certified automotive
training programs.

National Institute for Automotive Service Excellence (ASE)

www.ase.com
Find out more about being an auto technician.

INDEX

About the Author

Chris Jozefowicz studied to be a scientist but ended up as a writer. He has written scientific papers, medical reports, news stories, magazine articles, and video game reviews. Today, he mainly writes articles about science. He lives in Louisville, Kentucky, with his wife, their daughter, and their car.